LEGENDARY
STAR-LORD

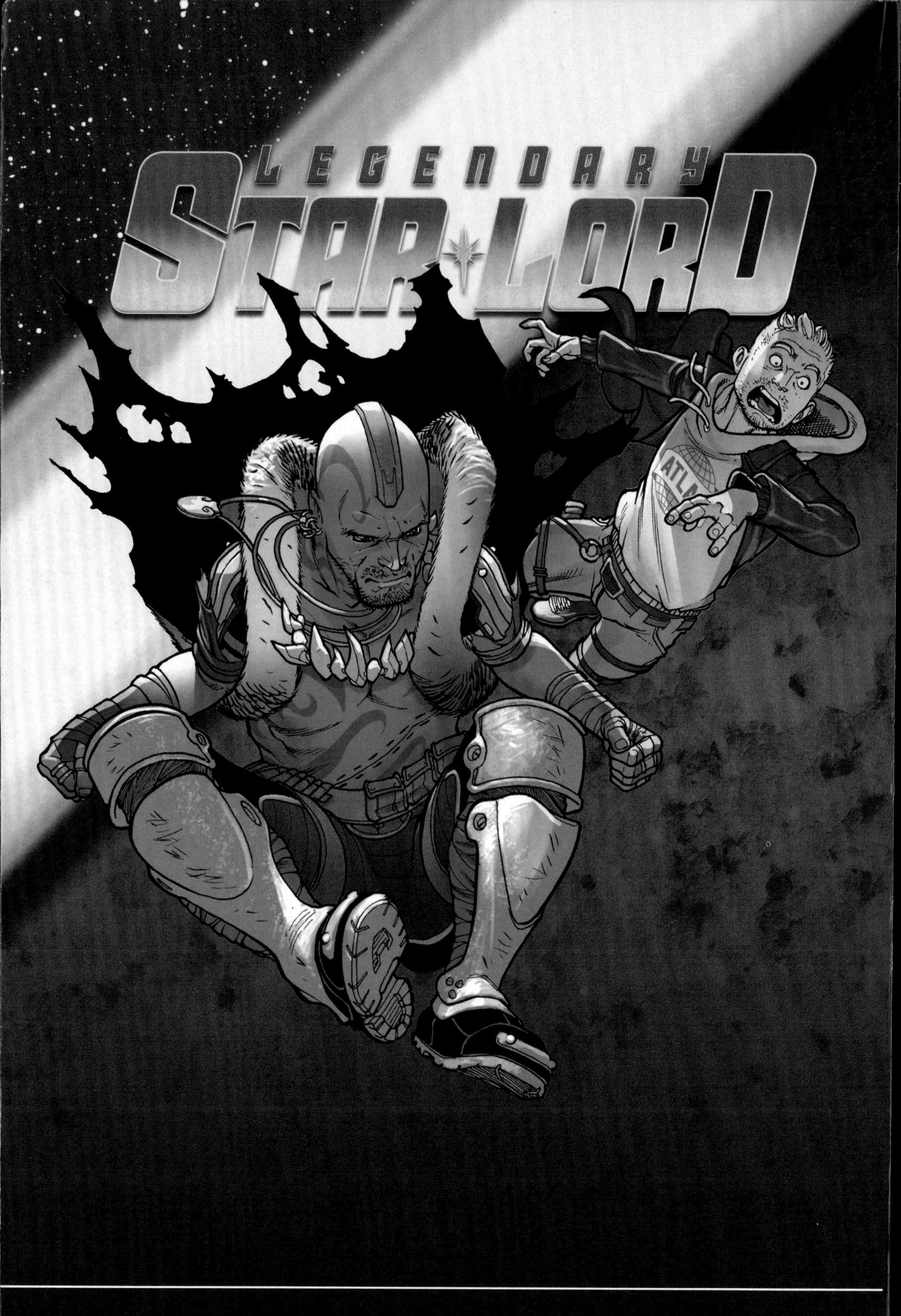

LEGENDARY STAR-LORD VOL. 3: FIRST FLIGHT. Contains material originally published in magazine form as STAR-LORD #1-5. First printing 2016. ISBN# 978-0-7851-9624-2. Published by MARVEL WORLDWIDE, INC., a subsidiary of MARVEL ENTERTAINMENT, LLC. OFFICE OF PUBLICATION: 135 West 50th Street, New York, NY 10020. **Printed in Canada.** ALAN FINE, President, Marvel Entertainment; DAN BUCKLEY, President, TV, Publishing & Brand Management; JOE QUESADA, Chief Creative Officer; TOM BREVOORT, SVP of Publishing; DAVID BOGART, SVP of Business Affairs & Operations, Publishing & Partnership; C.B. CEBULSKI, VP of Brand Management & Development, Asia; DAVID GABRIEL, SVP of Sales & Marketing, Publishing; JEFF YOUNGQUIST, VP of Production & Special Projects; DAN CARR, Executive Director of Publishing Technology; ALEX MORALES, Director of Publishing Operations; SUSAN CRESPI, Production Manager; STAN LEE, Chairman Emeritus. For information regarding advertising in Marvel Comics or on Marvel.com, please contact Vit DeBellis, Integrated Sales Manager, at vdebellis@marvel.com. For Marvel subscription inquiries, please call 888-511-5480. **Manufactured between 4/29/2016 and 6/6/2016 by SOLISCO PRINTERS, SCOTT, QC, CANADA.**

10 9 8 7 6 5 4 3 2 1

FIRST FLIGHT

WRITER: **SAM HUMPHRIES**

ARTIST: **JAVIER GARRÓN**

COLORISTS: **ANTONIO FABELA** WITH **FRANK D'ARMATA** (#1)

LETTERER: **VC'S JOE CARAMAGNA**

COVER ART: **DAVE JOHNSON**

ASSISTANT EDITOR: **KATHLEEN WISNESKI**

EDITOR: **JAKE THOMAS**

COLLECTION EDITOR: **SARAH BRUNSTAD**
ASSOCIATE MANAGING EDITOR: **ALEX STARBUCK**
EDITORS, SPECIAL PROJECTS:
MARK D. BEAZLEY & JENNIFER GRÜNWALD
VP, PRODUCTION & SPECIAL PROJECTS: **JEFF YOUNGQUIST**
SVP PRINT, SALES & MARKETING: **DAVID GABRIEL**
BOOK DESIGNER: **JAY BOWEN**

EDITOR IN CHIEF: **AXEL ALONSO**
CHIEF CREATIVE OFFICER: **JOE QUESADA**
PUBLISHER: **DAN BUCKLEY**
EXECUTIVE PRODUCER: **ALAN FINE**

ONE

YEAR ONE, CHAPTER ONE: FREE FALLING

GO WASH UP FOR DINNER, PETER.
RAIN IS COMING.
I WAS TEN YEARS OLD THE FIRST TIME I SAW AN ALIEN.
IT WAS NOT A GOOD EXPERIENCE.
MOM!
MY MOM GAVE HER LIFE TO GIVE ME A CHANCE.

EIGHT YEARS LATER...

BEEP

BEEP

BEEP

WARNING.

SO YOU MAY BE ASKING YOURSELF--

WHY DIDN'T I BECOME A VETERINARIAN?
ENEMY SHIPS CLOSING IN RAPIDLY.
I KNOW, I KNOW!
BEEP BEEP BEEP
BEEP BEEP

THEY ARE FASTER THAN YOU.
I KNOW, I KNOW!
LET'S SEE LET'S SEE--
DANGER
WARNING
YOU'RE HIGH ON HEAT BUT LOW ON COMPRESSION, YOUR IONS ARE UP BUT THE DEUTRONIUM IS DOWN--
C'MON, WHAT DO YOU NEED?!
I'M SORRY, I'M AFRAID I CAN'T ANSWER THAT.
THIRTY SECONDS UNTIL IMPACT --
JUST GO FASTER, PLEASE?!
OH GOD, EENIE MEENIE MINEY...
...BLAST THE THRUSTERS! GO!
INCORRECT.
ENGINE STALL.
FWASHA BOOM
FATALITY.
YAAAAAGH--
HEY, PETEY, OPEN UP!

FREDDIE.
PLEASE LET ME DIE IN PEACE.
CAN IT, PETEY, IT'S ALMOST SIX IN THE MORNING!
I JUST NEED ONE MORE GO IN THE SIMULATOR, COVER FOR ME! PLEASE!
FLIGHT SIMULATOR
CAUTION
NO CAN DO, YOU'RE GONNA GET CAUGHT IF YOU DON'T GET A MOVE ON. YOU BEEN IN THAT TIN CAN ALL NIGHT?
YEAH...
WHENEVER I CAN SNEAK IN THE TIME.
WELL, WAKE UP, BUTTERCUP. WE GOT NINE SHIPS IN THE HANGAR WITH MAGNETOPLASMADYNAMIC THRUSTERS THAT NEED FIXIN'.
OH, YEAH-- HEYWOOD CALLED IN SICK. SO YOU GOTTA CLEAN THE FLOORS. HYUK HYUK HYUK!
OH.
GREAT.
HERE SHE IS.
MY ONLY SHIP.
IN ALL HER GLORY.
STARK INDUSTRIES

LONG BEACH, CALIFORNIA.
NASA OPS LAUNCH FACILITY.
YOU'D THINK--AFTER WHAT HAPPENED TO ME AS A KID--I'D RATHER VISIT THE DENTIST THAN OUTER SPACE.
YOU'D THINK I'D SUPER GLUE MY FEET TO THE GROUND.
YOU'D THINK I'D ABSOLUTELY, ONE HUNDRED PERCENT HATE SPACE.
WELL...THE OPPOSITE HAPPENED. I'M OBSESSED.
ONE DAY-- I'M GONNA FLY THAT BIG SHIP BACK THERE.
THE ASTERION ONE.
I'M GONNA BE THE GREATEST ASTRONAUT IN THE GALAXY.
IT'S JUST THAT NO ONE KNOWS IT YET.
HEY, WATCH IT, SCRUB!
HERE IT COMES!

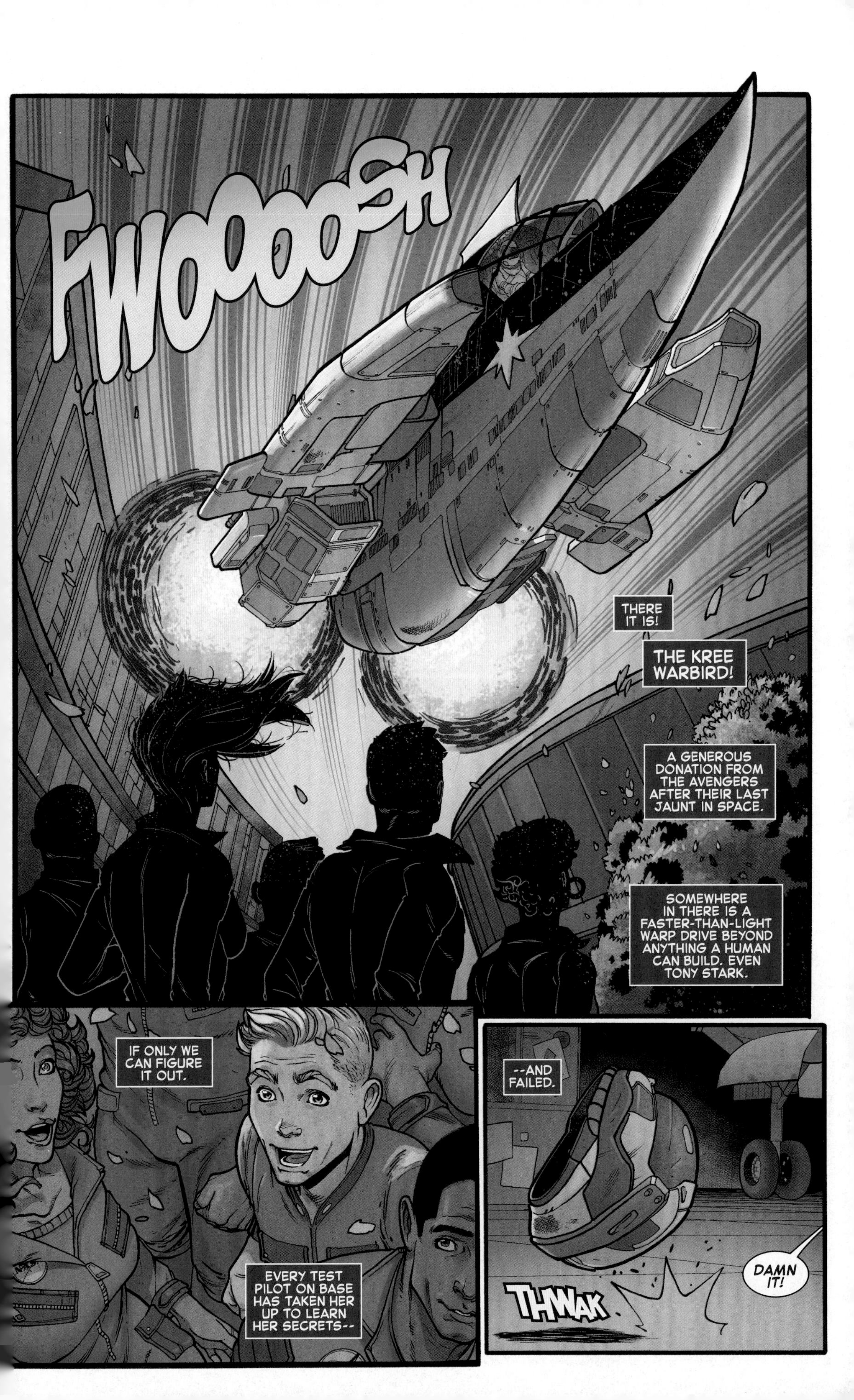
FWOOOOSH
THERE IT IS!
THE KREE WARBIRD!
A GENEROUS DONATION FROM THE AVENGERS AFTER THEIR LAST JAUNT IN SPACE.
SOMEWHERE IN THERE IS A FASTER-THAN-LIGHT WARP DRIVE BEYOND ANYTHING A HUMAN CAN BUILD. EVEN TONY STARK.
IF ONLY WE CAN FIGURE IT OUT.
EVERY TEST PILOT ON BASE HAS TAKEN HER UP TO LEARN HER SECRETS--
--AND FAILED.
THWAK
DAMN IT!

HASTINGS, TAKE CARE OF YOUR HELMET AND YOUR HELMET WILL TAKE CARE OF YOU--
SCREW MY HELMET.
YOU FAILED TO--
I TRIED THE QUANTUM DEFLECTORS.
YES, BUT THE AERO-SPIKE TURBINE...?
I PUSHED HER TO THE LIMIT.
I DID EVERYTHING I COULD THINK OF AND SHE STALLED!
NEVER ONCE HAD A BIRD STALL ON ME.
OFFICER BROCKMAN, SIR!
EASY NOW, HASTINGS. YOU'RE IN DISTINGUISHED COMPANY. NOT A SINGLE PILOT HAS BEEN ABLE TO DO WHAT YOU FAILED TO DO UP THERE.
YOU HEAR THAT, HOT SHOTS? HUMANITY NEEDS YOU AND YOU ARE BLOWING IT.
THERE'S A WARP DRIVE HIBERNATING IN THERE, JUST WAITING TO BE FOUND.
WITHOUT ITS SECRETS, THE ASTERION ONE IS GONNA BE AS USELESS AS A BATHTUB IN THE INDY 500.
WE'RE BACK TO SQUARE ONE. IDEAS?
ISNT'S IT OBVIOUS?
DROP THE HAMMER ON THE THRUSTERS. FORCE THAT DRIVE TO WAKE UP.
THAT'S A DUMB IDEA.

IF SHE'S STALLING, THEN MAYBE STOP PUSHING HER SO HARD.
INSTEAD OF GUNNING THE WARBIRD UNTIL SHE BLEEDS, PULL UP TO ESCAPE VELOCITY, AND CUT THE THRUSTERS! JUST FOR A SECOND--
THAT WILL FREE UP IONS TO THE FASTER-THAN-LIGHT DRIVE, AND BOOM!
WARP SPEED, BABY!
YEAH, OR GO BACK TO IGNORING ME...
HM, THE IONS--?
"CUT THE THRUSTERS?!" THAT IS THE SINGLE MOST IDIOTIC THING I'VE EVER HEARD!
GOING SLOWER IS THE OPPOSITE GOAL OF WARP DRIVE, DIPSTICK!

SHE'S A PRECISION INSTRUMENT, STOP DRIVING HER LIKE A SLEDGE-HAMMER!
GET BACK TO YOUR VACUUM, SCRUB! THE REAL PILOTS ARE TALKING!
WHEN A REAL PILOT STARTS TALKING, LET ME KNOW, JACKASS.
STEP INTO MY OFFICE, WHY DON'TCHA?

THAT'S ENOUGH!
ISAAC, GO OVER YOUR FLIGHT PLAN!
YOU! MECHANIC! GO...DO WHATEVER YOU'RE SUPPOSED TO BE DOING!
THAT'S RIGHT, GREASE MONKEY!
YOU DON'T HAVE WHAT IT TAKES TO BE AN ASTRONAUT!

KRAK

LATER.
LISA--?
THAT'S COMMANDER CHANG WHEN YOU'RE ON MY BOAT.
YOU ARE PUTTING ME IN A TERRIBLE POSITION, PETER.
COMMANDER CHANG... YOU WANTED TO SEE ME?
HEY, HE ASKED FOR IT.
I'M TALKING ABOUT HUNDREDS OF UNAUTHORIZED HOURS IN THE SIMULATORS.
OH! NEVER MIND WHAT I SAID!
SO WHAT DO YOU THINK OF MY FLYING? PRETTY SLICK, HUH? DO I GET THE JOB OR WHAT?
NO. YOU DEFINITELY DO NOT "GET" THE JOB.
LOOK AT THIS SHIP, PETER. WE'RE GOING TO BE THE FIRST MISSION TO COLONIZE ANOTHER PLANET--DO YOU THINK WE HAVE ANY ROOM FOR WILD CARDS?
IF YOU'RE EVER GOING TO--YOU KNOW WHAT, FORGET IT.

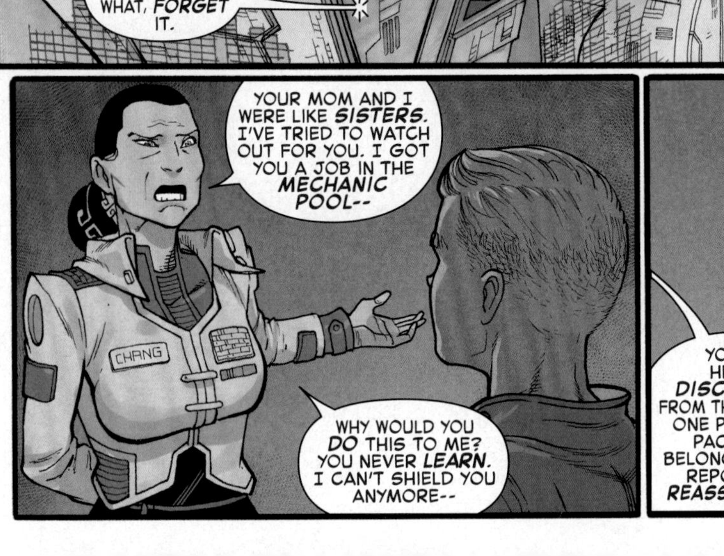
YOUR MOM AND I WERE LIKE SISTERS. I'VE TRIED TO WATCH OUT FOR YOU. I GOT YOU A JOB IN THE MECHANIC POOL--
WHY WOULD YOU DO THIS TO ME? YOU NEVER LEARN. I CAN'T SHIELD YOU ANYMORE--

YOU ARE HEREBY DISCHARGED FROM THE ASTERION ONE PROGRAM. PACK YOUR BELONGINGS AND REPORT FOR REASSIGNMENT.
WHAT-- BUT MY FLYING--
I'M SORRY, LISA, I JUST--
I WANT TO BE AN ASTRONAUT--!

PETER, YOU DO NOT UNDERSTAND WHAT IT MEANS TO BE AN ASTRONAUT!
SNEAKING AROUND, LYING-- SOLVING ARGUMENTS WITH YOUR FISTS!
WHAT WOULD YOUR MOTHER SAY?
KRBASH
PETER...!
COMMANDER CHANG? WE NEED YOU OVER HERE FOR A MOMENT--

ASTERION ONE
EXTERNAL BOLT HATCH
CHAMPION
CONCERT
THIS WAS MY BIG CHANCE.
GO!
THE SHIP THAT KILLED MY MOM.
HOW AM I GONNA FIND IT NOW?
MY MOM GAVE HER LIFE TO GIVE ME A CHANCE.
ALL I HAVE TO DO IS NOT BLOW IT.
PICK A HIGH TARGET AND YOU WILL HIT IT, PETER.
WHAT IF I--
DON'T WORRY. I'M NOT GONNA BLOW THIS.

ELSEWHERE.
AH, SPACE.
A PLACE OF UNLIMITED POSSIBILITIES.
INFINITE WONDERS AND PRECIOUS MIRACLES--
--FOR ME TO ROB, CHEAT, AND STEAL.
BOSS! THAT KREE WARBIRD YOU WANTED-- IT'S BACK ONLINE!
TRACK IT--AND IF YOU LOSE IT AGAIN, I'LL LEAVE YOU HIGH AND DRY!
YES, SIR!
FINALLY--
"--THAT LITTLE LOST BIRD IS GONNA BE OURS."
ASTERION ONE...YOU'RE THE MOST BEAUTIFUL SHIP I'VE EVER SEEN--

BUT YOU ARE OVER BUDGET, OVER SCHEDULE...AND IT'S MY FAULT.
AN OFF-WORLD COLONY. FOR GENERATIONS, HUMANS HAVE DREAMED OF THIS. WELL, THE NERDY ONES, AT LEAST.
AND ME. I'VE STAKED EVERYTHING ON THIS MISSION, AND NOW IT'S ABOUT TO FALL APART--

DIRECTOR CHANG, WE HAVE A TWELVE-DELTA EMERGENCY--
AN UNAUTHORIZED LAUNCH?

IT'S THE KREE WARBIRD!
YOOOOOOO--!
FWOOOOSH
CENTCOM HAS BEEN ALERTED, THEY'RE ACTIVATING SECURITY PROTOCOLS--
PETER!
THEY'LL SHOOT HIM OUT OF THE SKY--!

PETER QUILL! THIS IS CENTCOM, WE KNOW YOU'RE IN THERE!
YOU ARE IN POSSESSION OF STOLEN ALIEN TECHNOLOGY!
SURRENDER YOUR AIRCRAFT OR WE WILL BRING YOU DOWN!
THE MECHANIC FROM THIS MORNING? HE'S GONNA KILL HIMSELF!
THAT'S MY BIRD, DAMMIT!
UH, NEGATIVE, CHAIR JOCKIES. THIS IS TONY STARK, JUST TAKING HER OUT FOR A SPIN, HOPE YOU DON'T MIND!
I AM VERY RICH, YOU KNOW!
MESSAGE RECEIVED. WARNING FIRE AUTHORIZED.
FZZZK
FZZZK
FWASHKABASH

NO WAY, EVERYONE LOVES MY TONY STARK IMPRESSION!

CENTCOM, THIS IS **COMMANDER CHANG! HOLD FIRE!** REPEAT, DO **NOT** FIRE ON HIM!

SORRY, COMMANDER, PROTOCOLS REQUIRE RUNAWAY ALIEN TECH MUST BE NEUTRALIZED--**ZERO TOLERANCE**--

PETER!

BYE BYE, BUSTERS.

HEY, THERE'S KELLY!

PAGE ME LATER, KELLY!

FWOOOOOSH

NO WAY, THEY'RE STILL RIGHT ON MY BUTT!

C'MON, QUILL, GIVE 'EM SOMETHING GOOD, A TRICK THEY'VE NEVER SEEN BEFORE--!

TARGET LOCKED!

YOU HAVE PERMISSION TO **BRING DOWN** THE WARBIRD.

LET'S SEE LET'S SEE--
HIGH ON HEAT. LOW ON COMPRESSION. IONS UP. DEUTRONIUM IS DOWN--
C'MON, WHAT DO YOU NEED?!
DON'T BLOW IT, QUILL!
OH GOD, EENIE MEENIE MINEY...
CUT THE THRUSTERS! DO IT!
HE CUT HIS THRUSTERS, HE'S SLOWING DOWN! TARGET ALMOST IN RANGE!
WE GOT HIM NOW-- HUH?!

UH-- COMMAND--
WE LOST THE TARGET, REPEAT--
THAT THING JUST DISAPPEARED!
THE TELEMETRY--! I CAN'T BELIEVE IT!
PETER DID IT! THE WARP DRIVE IS ONLINE!
WE GOT THE DATA! ASTERION ONE LIVES!
YEEEEE HAAAAAAW!
I DID IT! I DID IT--
I'M IN SPACE!
SUCK IT, EVERYONE ON EARTH!

KAR-KUNG
WHOA-A-A!
"KAR-KUNG?"
WE'RE NOT MOVING...?
NO...NO... THIS IS NOT HAPPENING.

NOTHING RESPONDING--
I'M SORRY, I DIDN'T MEAN TO--JUST WAKE UP, PLEASE--

PLEASE, BABY, DO THIS ONE THING FOR ME, AND--
I PROMISE I'LL TREAT YOU RIGHT, I'LL TAKE YOU OUT TO DINNER, DANCING, WHATEVER YOU WANT--
NO THRUST, NO IONS, NO COMPRESSION, NO RESPONSE--

PLEASE.

BANG BANG BANG
DON'T DO THIS TO ME--

GREAT.

I'M TOTALLY
BLOWING IT.

TWO YEAR ONE, CHAPTER TWO: SPACE PIRATES OF THE GALAXY

FIRST TIME I TRAVELED TO SPACE, EVERYTHING WENT ACCORDING TO PLAN.
THAT WAS SO FUN!
SPACE PIRATES OF THE GALAXY
ENTRANCE
STAFF
EXCEPT THE CONSTELLATIONS WERE REVERSED AND THERE'S NO SOUND IN SPACE AND--
MONICA! IT'S JUST A RIDE!
SPACE IS COOL.
SPACE IS COOL, PETER.
SPACE PIRATES OF THE GALAXY
I'M GONNA BE AN ASTRONAUT AND FLY MY OWN SHIP AND--
BUT IF I'M BEING HONEST--THIS TIME I HAD NO PLAN.
MOM--?! LOOK! THE SPACE PIRATE--
BACKSTAGE AREA
Space Flight Crew Only!
--HE'S JUST A GUY!
OPCORN
SO WHAT THE HELL AM I DOING OUT HERE?

DRIFTING IN SPACE.
THREE DAYS NOW.
BANGING MY HEAD AGAINST THIS ENGINE.
IT'S PRETENDING TO BE BROKEN JUST TO SPITE ME, I KNOW IT.
COME ON!
REVEAL TO ME YOUR SECRETS!
TALK TO ME!
HELLOOO?
UH-- HELLO?
TO WHOM AM I SPEAKING?
...PETER QUILL?
HELLO THERE, PETER QUILL.
I'VE LOST IT.
LOOKS LIKE YOU'RE HAVING MECHANICAL PROBLEMS.
OH-- WHAT--HEY! OH MY GOD, HELLO!
SORRY, I THOUGHT I WAS TALKING TO--UH, NEVER MIND THAT!
THANK YOU, THANK YOU! I THOUGHT I'D NEVER GET RESCUED!
OH, WE'RE NOT HERE TO RESCUE YOU--

WE'RE PIRATES.
WE STEAL THINGS.
PREPARE TO BE BOARDED.

DO AS I SAY, MISTER QUILL, AND YOU'LL COME OUT OF THIS WITH ALL YOUR FINGERS AND TENTACLES AND TOES.
BUT GIVE US ANY TROUBLE--
TENTACLES?!
WHO ARE THESE GUYS?!
WE JUST WANT YOUR SHIP, THEN WE'LL BE ON OUR MERRY WAY.
NO WAY! I STOLE THIS SHIP FIRST!
THINK, PETER, THINK...
NOW, HAVE A SEAT AND DON'T GO DEVELOPING ANY NERVOUS TICS--
NICE AND EASY, YEAH?
HOLD ON TIGHT--
THEY'RE HERE--

YOU'RE ABOUT TO BE ROBBED BY YONDU AND THE RAVAGERS!

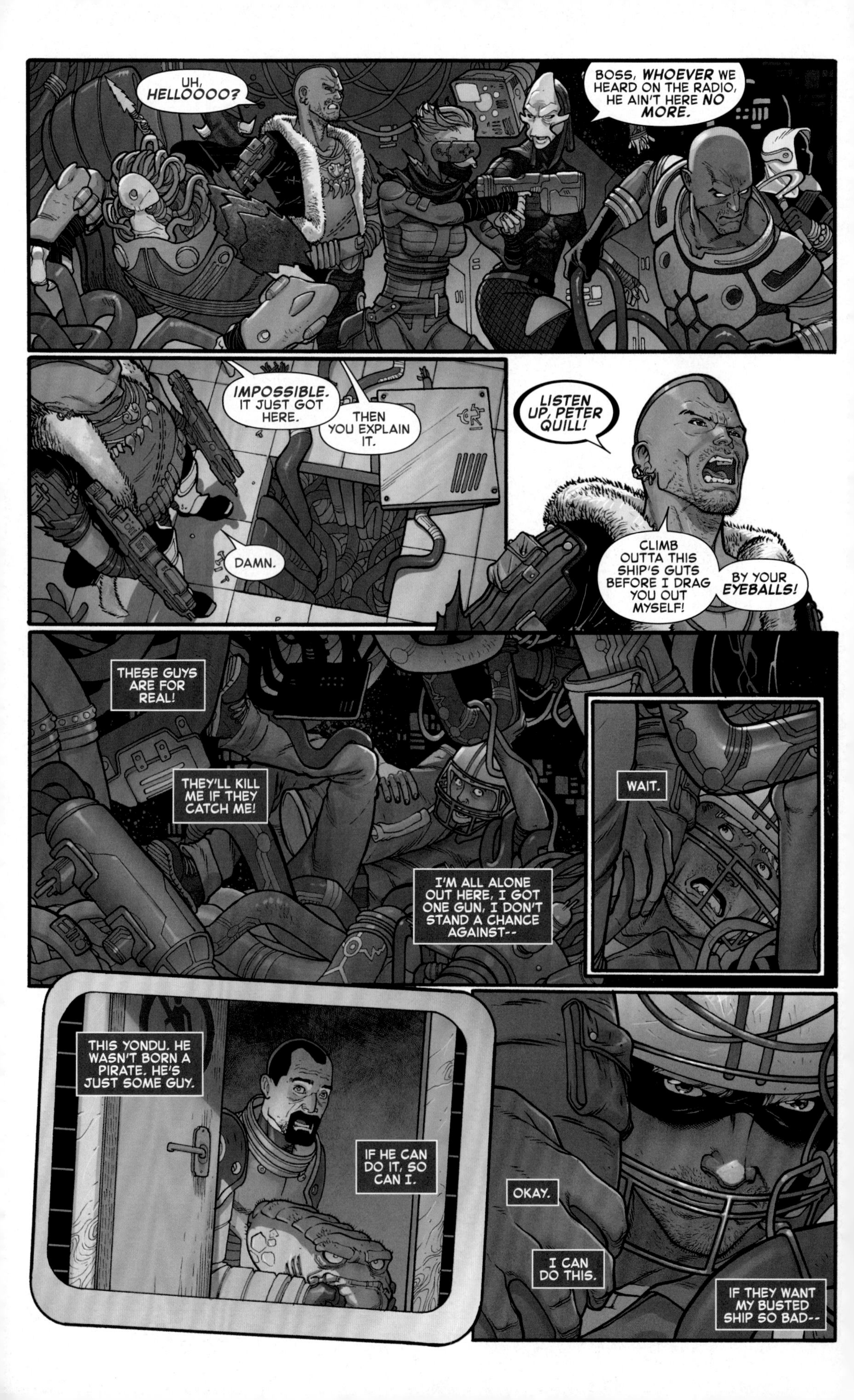
UH, HELLOOOO?
BOSS, WHOEVER WE HEARD ON THE RADIO, HE AIN'T HERE NO MORE.
IMPOSSIBLE. IT JUST GOT HERE.
THEN YOU EXPLAIN IT.
DAMN.
LISTEN UP, PETER QUILL!
CLIMB OUTTA THIS SHIP'S GUTS BEFORE I DRAG YOU OUT MYSELF!
BY YOUR EYEBALLS!
THESE GUYS ARE FOR REAL!
THEY'LL KILL ME IF THEY CATCH ME!
I'M ALL ALONE OUT HERE, I GOT ONE GUN, I DON'T STAND A CHANCE AGAINST--
WAIT.
THIS YONDU. HE WASN'T BORN A PIRATE. HE'S JUST SOME GUY.
IF HE CAN DO IT, SO CAN I.
OKAY.
I CAN DO THIS.
IF THEY WANT MY BUSTED SHIP SO BAD--

--THEY CAN HAVE IT.
KLANK
DEAR COMPUTER, SIMULATE A LITTLE RADIATION LEAK, AND--
TAKAKAKA
THE DOOR SEALED SHUT!
KLAM
WHAT THE--?!
HEY, WHERE'S YONDU?
AH HA.
VERY CLEVER, "PETER QUILL"--
WHOEVER YOU ARE.
IMPROVISE, PETER! IMPROVISE!
WAIT-- IS THAT WHAT I THINK IT IS?

RRRRURMBLRLRE
HANG ON!
WHO STARTED THIS THING?
WE'RE TRAPPED IN HERE--
I'D KNOW A BULLDOZER ANYWHERE IN THE GALAXY!
YEEEEE HAAAAAAW!
SKREEEEEEE
WALK THE PLANK, SUCKERS!
FEEL FREE TO TAKE MY SHIP--

I'LL JUST TAKE YOURS INSTEAD!
THIS SHIP IS THE PROPERTY OF PETER QUILL!
KING OF ALL PIRATES!
NOW, I KNOW WHAT YOU'RE THINKING--
STEALING SPACESHIPS IS HOW I GOT INTO THIS MESS IN THE FIRST PLACE.
BUT I'VE GOT A GOOD FEELING ABOUT THIS.
YEAH, THIS IS GONNA WORK OUT JUST--
WHOOMPH!
WHOOMPH

I'M GONNA PULL OUT YOUR LUNGS AND--
YAAAAH!
I DIDN'T MEAN IT--
PETER! YOUR GUN! FIRE!
FIRE.
FRATAKIN'--
THAT HURT!
GREAT, NOW HE'S JUST PISSED.
OKAY, PLAN A SUCKED.
AND I DON'T HAVE A PLAN B.
QUILL! HOW LONG YOU THINK YOU GONNA HIDE FROM ME IN MY OWN SHIP?!
UH...WELP, YONDU, YOU'VE GOT A POINT.
OH... WOW.
HOW DO YOU OUTWIT A PIRATE IN HIS OWN SHIP?

THE LONGER YOU WAIT, THE WORSE IT'S GONNA BE FOR YA!
KLANG KLANG KLANG
I HEAR YOU, QUILL! YOU'RE SCURRYING OFF INTO--
YOU GOTTA GET UNDER HIS SKIN.
AND WHAT DOES A PIRATE CARE ABOUT MORE THAN ANYTHING ELSE?
HELL NO, I SAY HELL NO!
YOU GOT SOME GUTS ON YOU! KICKING OFF MY CREW IS ONE THING. STEALING MY SHIP IS ANOTHER!
BUT THE DEVIL I'M GONNA LET YOU GET UP CLOSE WITH MY--
TREASURE.
LOOT.
BOOTY.
I SEE YOU, QUILL!

NO WAY OUT! PUT YOUR HANDS UP AND EMPTY YOUR POCKETS!
COME ON, COME ON--
PUSH!
IF YOU TRY TO STEAL SO MUCH AS ONE SHI'AR GOLD TOOTH--
OH, NO.
KREEEEEK
YOU WANNA MAKE A PIRATE DO SOMETHING STUPID, LIKE RUSH INTO A TRAP?
NO--!
HIT HIM WHERE IT HURTS.
THUNK

...THANOS... GET BACK HERE... GONNA KICK YOUR ASS...
NNNNF. QUILL.
GONNA... KEEEL YOU.
HUH. YOU ACTUALLY TOOK THE TIME TO DRESS MY WOUND.
THAT WAS STUPID.
YEAH, THAT BURN LOOKED PRETTY BAD.
HEY, WANNA TELL ME WHERE THE IGNITION IS ON MY BRAND-NEW SHIP?
AIN'T YOUR SHIP.
THAT'S COOL, I'LL FIGURE IT OUT IN FIVE MINUTES.
GIVE UP NOW, QUILL.
DON'T BE A SORE LOSER. THERE'S NO WAY OUT FOR YOU.

I GUESS YOU THOUGHT OF EVERYTHING, EH?
TELL ME, QUILL, WHAT'S A DIRT APE EARTHMAN DOING ALL THE WAY OUT HERE?

CAN YOU JUST TELL ME IF I'M GETTING WARMER, OR--?
OH YEAH.

YER REAL HOT!
KRSSSSH
FWOOPH!
YOU THINK YOU CAN KEEP ME A PRISONER IN MY OWN HANDCUFFS?
THINK AGAIN, YOU--
HOLY FLAKNARDS!

YOU'RE A KID?!
PLAN C!
PLAN C!
KA-KIK
I'M A KID WITH A GUN.
PLAN C IS... WORK THAT PETER QUILL CHARM!

KID, I'VE KEELHAULED MEN MORE DECENT THAN YOU FOR BEIN' LESS OBNOXIOUS.
HERE'S THE DEAL: YOU PUT YOUR GUN DOWN QUIETLY, WE TAKE WHAT WE WANT FROM YOUR SHIP AND SCUTTLE IT. LET YOU DRIFT.
WE PUT YOUR FATE IN THE HANDS OF THE STARS.
HIGH AND DRY. THE PIRATE WAY.
SOUNDS LIKE A STUPID DEAL.
IT'S BETTER ODDS THAN YOU'RE ABOUT TO HAVE IN FIVE SECONDS.
I MEAN-- KINDA STUPID TO SET ME ADRIFT WHEN I COULD BE USEFUL TO YOU.
YOU SHOULD MAKE ME A MEMBER OF YOUR CREW.
HA. HA.
FOUR SECONDS.
I TRAPPED YOUR FRIENDS, STOLE YOUR SHIP, FOUND YOUR TREASURE, AND ALMOST GOT AWAY WITH IT!
YOU AIN'T EXACTLY INGRATIATING YOURSELF HERE, QUILL.
THREE.

I GOT YOU OVER A BARREL. NOT MANY PEOPLE CAN DO THAT, CAN THEY?
YOU'RE JUST A DIRT BOY FROM EARTH. NOT ONE OF YOU IS WORTH A DAMN OUT HERE IN SPACE.
TWO.
THAT SHIP YOU STOLE FROM ME? I STOLE IT FIRST! I KILLED AN ALIEN WHEN I WAS TEN!
PEOPLE SAID I DIDN'T HAVE WHAT IT TAKES TO GO INTO SPACE, BUT I PROVED THEM WRONG!
ONE.
PLEASE.
I DON'T HAVE ANYWHERE ELSE TO GO.
"EARTH SALUTES YOU!"

HUMANITY'S HOPES FOR THE FUTURE REST ON YOUR SHOULDERS!
YOU CARRY YOUR CREW AND OUR DREAMS TO THE STARS!
ASTERION ONE!
A MISSION TO ESTABLISH A HUMAN COLONY ON ANOTHER PLANET!
LO, THE MANY GENERATIONS HAVE GAZED AT THE STARS AND--
SHUT THAT OFF, BROCKMAN. WE'RE JUST DOING A MISSION HERE. NOTHING MORE.
AYE, COMMANDER CHANG.
ALL STATIONS ARE GO. READY FOR YOUR WORD. WOULD YOU LIKE TO COUNT DOWN?
I'D RATHER CONSERVE THE OXYGEN. HASTINGS AND ISAAC-- YOU ARE CLEAR.
AYE AYE, COMMANDER CHANG!
INITIATING WARP DRIVE!
FUNNY...
COMMANDER?
WE'D NEVER KNOW HOW TO UNLOCK THE WARP DRIVE IF IT WEREN'T FOR PETER. AND I SAID HE DIDN'T HAVE WHAT IT TAKES...
I WONDER IF HE'S STILL ALIVE OUT THERE?
I KNOW YOU WERE CLOSE WITH HIS MOTHER.
ALL HANDS PREPARE FOR WARP!

ASTERION ONE, YOU ARE CLEAR FOR WARP--
LAUNCH!
WARP LAUNCH SUCCESSFUL!
GODSPEED, ASTERION ONE!
"HE ALMOST KILLED US ALL, YONDU."

HE DIDN'T "ALMOST" KILL YOU, PUSHOVER. HE LEFT YOU HIGH AND DRY. IT IS THE PIRATE WAY...
SO WHAT THE HELL IS HE STILL BREATHING FOR?
YOUR HOME PLANET?
YOU EVER BEEN TO CENTAURI IV?
DAMN BEAUTIFUL PLACE. PARADISE IN THE OUTER SPIRAL ARM OF THE GALAXY.

I WAS ALWAYS A LITTLE TOO ROUGH AND TUMBLE FOR THAT CROWD. NOT MUCH FOR HUGGIN' TREES OR SINGIN' SONGS.
"YOU'LL NEVER MAKE A GOOD CENTAURIAN." THAT'S WHAT THEY TOLD ME...
RIGHT BEFORE THEY CUT OFF MY HEADFIN AND KICKED ME OFF THE PLANET.
I MISS THAT PLACE.
BEASTIES

THE KID IS ONE OF US. MAYBE ONE DAY HE'LL BE A GREAT PIRATE.
OR MAYBE WE'LL JUST LET HIM CLEAN THE SHIP.
HEY KID! YOU MISSED A SPOT!
BEASTIES
WHEN I SAID I COULD BE USEFUL, THIS IS NOT WHAT I HAD IN MIND.

WELCOME TO MY "NEW" JOB.
FOR NOW.
I'M GONNA WATCH, AND I'M GONNA LEARN.
I'M GOING TO BE A PIRATE.
IF THESE GUYS CAN DO IT, THEN SO CAN I.
Star-Lord

#2 VARIANT BY KOI CARREON

THREE

YEAR ONE, CHAPTER THREE: INTO THE GREAT WIDE OPEN

IT'S MORE BEAUTIFUL THAN I THOUGHT.

I BUSTED MY ASS FOR THIS VIEW. I GOT OFF EARTH, FOUND A NEW CREW. ALL BY MYSELF.

NOW I NEED TO FIGURE OUT HOW TO STOP PUSHING A VACUUM CLEANER...

SOMEBODY'S *SLEEPIN'.*

YONDU!
SOMEBODY'S TAKIN' A LITTLE NAP. INSTEAD OF CLEANIN' MY FLOORS.
YEAH-- I MEAN-- NO!
I WAS JUST CLEANING THE GLASS, CZAR KEEPS LEAVING SMUDGES ALL OVER-- I MEAN--
WHAT'RE YOU LOOKIN' AT THAT'S MORE IMPORTANT THAN MY FLOORS, PETEY?
BEASTIES
AH, OF COURSE. THE BADOON SHIP YOU'RE LOOKING FOR. THE ONE YOU ASKED ME TO FIND FOR YOU.
A HUNDRED TIMES.
SATOOM PHOTO
HOW ABOUT A HUNDRED AND ONE?
LET ME ASK YOU SOMETHING, KID.
WHAT WOULD YOU DO IF YOU EVEN FOUND IT?
SHOOT IT OUT OF THE SKY.
THROW IT INTO THE SUN.
PEE ON THE ASHES.
DANCE ON ITS GRAVE.
PETEY, YOU'RE GONNA GET YOURSELF KILLED THINKING STUPID LIKE THAT.
HERE'S THE THING ABOUT SPACE, EARTH BOY-- IT AIN'T COMPLICATED. IT'S ALL JUST THE BIG NOTHING OUT THERE.
VERY OCCASIONALLY PUNCTUATED BY SOMETHING OF INTEREST. COULD BE TREASURE...
OR IT COULD BE SOMETHING THAT THREATENS TO TAKE THE AIR OUTTA YOUR LUNGS.
BEASTIES

STEAL ONE. AVOID THE OTHER.
BUT--
THAT'S IT. THAT'S THE BIG SECRET ABOUT SPACE.
BUT--
NO BUTS!
BEASTIES
YEAH, BUT, LOOK--
THAT'S ME, MY MOM MEREDITH, AND MY MOM'S BEST FRIEND LISA.
THE BADOON IN THAT SHIP KILLED MY MOM AND LEFT ME ALONE FOREVER.
WAS YOUR MOM A PIRATE?
DOES SHE LOOK LIKE A PIRATE?
LISA BECAME A SHIP COMMANDER, THOUGH. COURSE, SHE'D NEVER HAVE GOTTEN THOSE FOUR WARP DRIVES OPERATIONAL IF I HADN'T FIGURED THEM OUT.
AN EARTHER SHIP WITH FOUR WARP DRIVES?
HELL YEAH! REVERSE ENGINEERED FROM THE KREE, AND I CRACKED 'EM. I KNOW ALL THE INS AND OUTS. ALL THE SECRETS.
I MAKE A MUCH BETTER MECHANIC THAN A JANITOR, YOU KNOW!
OR MAYBE... A PIRATE?
YOU DON'T SAY...

BUT I HATE THE ASTERION'S CREW. THEY TREATED ME LIKE A CHUMP. SAID THEY'D NEVER LET ME BE AN ASTRONAUT. SAID I COULD NEVER CUT IT IN SPACE.
EASY NOW, PAL, THOSE DAYS ARE LONG GONE! YOU'RE AMONG FRIENDS!
I AM?
AS FAR AS I UNDERSTAND THE CONCEPT! NOW LISTEN, YOUNG TIGER--
YOU'VE BEEN LOCKED UP IN HERE MOPPING FLOORS FOR TOO LONG.
MAYBE YOU'RE RIGHT. MAYBE YOU DO HAVE WHAT IT TAKES TO BE A PIRATE!
IS HE SERIOUS?
BEASTIE
WHAT SAY WE GET OFF THIS SHIP, SEE THE GALAXY, CAUSE SOME TROUBLE?
THAT IS, IF YOU THINK YOU'RE READY... FOR SPACE.
SERIOUSLY?
HE'S SERIOUS!
THIS IS MY CHANCE!
OH MY GOD, PETER--DON'T BLOW THIS!

PLANETSIDE.
I THINK I'M BLOWING THIS.
ATL
GRRRRROWR
LET ME TELL YA' A LITTLE STORY, YONDU--

ONE TIME ON SIGMA 6 I GET A CONTRACT TO ROB SOME GEM REFINERIES.
ONLY MY PARTNER BRINGS SOME NEW GUY AROUND. A SNEEZY LITTLE SKEEZER.
"HE'S COOL, MAN, HE'S WITH ME! HE'S LIKE A LITTLE LOST PUPPY!"

JACQUES, PETER CAN'T HURT A FLY--LET'S JUST DO THE DEAL--
TURNS OUT, THE SNEEZY LITTLE SKEEZER WASN'T "COOL" AT ALL! AND I SPENT THE NEXT THIRTY YEARS IN A SPARTAX SOLAR PRISON!
SO PLEASE TAKE ME SERIOUSLY WHEN I SAY, NO NEW GUYS!

GROOOWLGH!
NO WAY OUT EXCEPT--

JACQUES, RELAX, PETER'S PART OF MY CREW! YOU'RE GONNA LOVE HIM--
I GOT YOUR MONEY, JUST GIVE ME THE GEM--
DON'T YOU TELL ME WHO I'M GONNA LOVE!
NO.
NOPE.
NO WAY.
THIRTY YEARS IN A SOLAR PRISON! WATCHIN' FROM AFAR AS MY KIDS CALL SOME OTHER BASTARD "DAD"--
NO! HEY! NOOOO.

WHOA--
AAA!
HELP!
GROOCH--?
SKONK
GROAAAWL!
I DIDN'T
MEAN IT!
WHAT THE
HELL--?
PETEY, I BRING YOU ON THE MOST PRIMITIVE FLARKIN' PICK-UP JOB AND YOU STILL BLOW IT--

ENOUGH!
THWAK
HEY!
I KNEW THIS WAS A SETUP! YOU TRYIN' TO RIP ME OFF--!
PETEY! STOP HIM!
DO WHAT NOW?
DON'T BLOW THIS--
HEY, UH--
FREEZE?
FAREWELL, SKEEZER--!
I BLEW IT.
FOLLOW 'IM!
FOLLOW HIM HOW?!

OH.
THIS IS HOW.
THWUMP
GET OFF MY BACK, YONDU!
OVER THERE!
JACQUES! GET BACK HERE--

WHOOMPH

I KNEW I SHOULD HAVE BLOCKED YOUR CALL! YOU'RE A LYING SON OF A KRUTAKER--
JUST HAND IT OVER, JACQUES.
THIS AIN'T A SCREW JOB, I SWEAR IT--
YAAAAUGH!
KA
FLAM
YA BASTARD--!
YOOOOR!

YOU WANT HELP?!
NO!
YOU SURE?!
GET THE OTHER GUY!
HUH?
DON'T BLOW IT THIS TIME.
DON'T BLOW IT.

KSSSSSH
HELP! I'M BEIN' ROBBED!
KHAAAK!
WHO? NO, I'M NOT--
?
!
PRASH
YEOOOW!
WHERE'S A FOOTBALL HELMET WHEN YOU NEED IT...?
ATLAS
YOU LET HIM GET AWAY?!

I DIDN'T--
HE DID--HE
ESCAPED--!
YOU PUSHOVER!
YOU IDIOT!
YOU'RE GOING STRAIGHT BACK TO THE SHIP--!
BUT-- WHEN I TACKLED HIM--I PICKPOCKETED THIS OUT OF HIS JACKET--
DID I DO GOOD?
PETEY...!
I'D SAY YOU DID BETTER THAN GOOD!
REALLY?
SO YOU'RE NOT GONNA SEND ME BACK TO THE SHIP?
ARE YOU KIDDING?
WE'RE JUST GETTING STARTED.
THAT'S THEM!
FREEZE! POLICE!

I'M DOING IT!
I'M NOT BLOWING IT!

I'M TOTALLY AWESOME!
BURP
THEK
OH, UH-- OUCH?
PSSST-- YOU EARNED IT.
THIS IS EMBARRASSING.
WHY, IT'S LIKE MONEY IN THE BANK!
C'MON, JOIN UP, AND I'LL BE FRANK!

UNLESS YOU DO, YOU'LL WALK THE PLAAAAANK!
AFTER FIRMANSYAH
YOU GOT THE GEM, CZAR?
YOU THINK IT WILL WORK?
JUST LOOK AT HIM. HE'S READY.
ALL RIGHT, QUIET DOWN, YOU MOLDY ROGUES!
QUIET, I SAID! SHADDUP! I GOT SOMETHING REAL IMPORTANT TO SAY!
AND IT'S ABOUT PETEY.
YOU CAME INTO OUR LIVES, AND WE INSTANTLY HATED YOUR GUTS.
HAHAHA
BUT SINCE THEN YOU'VE WON US OVER WITH YOUR EXUBERANCE AND CHARM. AND YOU'VE BECOME A PRETTY GOOD PIRATE--HEY, YOU'VE HAD THE BEST TEACHERS IN THE GALAXY!
AYE! AYEEE!
AW, HELL-- WHAT I'M TRYING TO SAY HERE, PETEY-- LET'S MAKE IT OFFICIAL.
WE'VE DECIDED TO MAKE YOU A FULL-TIME RAVAGER. WHADDYA SAY?
...
SERIOUSLY?

CLIK
SERIOUS AS A SKRULL. AND TO SEAL THE DEAL, WE GOT YOU A LITTLE GIFT.
THIS AIN'T NO ORDINARY PRECIOUS STONE, IT'S A TRACKING GEM. AND ON IT IS THE PRECISE LOCATION OF--
WHAT?
YOUR BADOON SPACE-SHIP.
I--
GUYS--
I DON'T KNOW WHAT TO SAY.
SAY YES, YOUNG TIGER! TAKE YOUR RIGHTFUL PLACE AMONGST THE STARS!
OH, THERE IS ONE THING. ONE LITTLE THING.
WE NEED YOU TO STEAL THE ASTERION ONE.

YOU NEED ME TO WHAT THE ASTERION ONE?
LISTEN UP, RAVAGERS! I GOT A NEW TARGET FOR US--HER NAME IS ASTERION ONE, NEWLY LAUNCHED FROM EARTH!
"SHE FLEW ACROSS A KYMELION PROBE DRONE--AND LUCKILY, I USED TO DATE THE KYMELION ON DUTY--SO GUESS WHO GOT THE INSIDE INFO?
"THE SHIP IS TAKING A HUNDRED EARTHLINGS FROM THEIR HOME MUD BALL TO SOME OTHER MUD BALL--
"I GUESS THEY'RE JUST GETTING AROUND TO SETTING UP THEIR FIRST OFF-WORLD COLONY. BLAH BLAH BLAH, BIG FLARKIN' DEAL. YAWN.
"BUT TO US, IT'S A FLYING BATHTUB FULL OF TREASURE!
"FOUR KREE-TECH WARP DRIVES, BIG ENOUGH TO POWER A COLONY-- AND NO WEAPONS ON BOARD.
"NICE AND FAT AND RIPE FOR THE STEALIN'."
BUT HOW WE GONNA TAKE IT, BOSS?
SIMPLE. PETEY HELPED BUILD THAT DANG THING. HE KNOWS ALL THE INS AND OUTS, ALL THE SECRETS!
HE'LL GET US IN NO PROBLEM.
RIIIIIGHT, PETEY?

WHAT? NO.
I DON'T WANNA DO THAT.
THE ASTERION ONE IS AWESOME! IT'S, LIKE, THE PINNACLE OF HUMAN ACHIEVEMENT. EVEN IF THE CREW IS A BUNCH OF JERKS--
ATLAS
BUUUUUT YOU'RE ONE OF US, NOW, RIGHT?
BESIDES, THOSE ASTERION ONE MUD APES DIDN'T BELIEVE IN YOU! YOU SAID SO YOURSELF.
THEY NEVER BELIEVED YOU COULD CUT IT IN SPACE. BUT WE DO. WE'RE GONNA MAKE YOU A RAVAGER.
WELL...
WHAT DO YOU CARE IF THEY BLOW THEIR DUMB MISSION? SCREW THOSE FLARKNARDS!
AND WE'LL GIVE YOU THIS, TOO. THE BADOON SHIP YOU WANNA CRUSH SO BAD. GET REVENGE FOR YOUR MOMMA.
DON'T YOU THINK IT'S A FAIR TRADE, PETEY? THE SHIP YOU WANT, FOR THE SHIP WE WANT!
I GUESS, BUT--
A TOAST--!
TO THE ASTERION ONE!
AND THE NEWEST MEMBER OF THE RAVAGERS!
ATLAS

TO PETEY QUILL!
DON'T BLOW IT, PETER. THIS IS YOUR BIG CHANCE.

#3 VARIANT BY CHRIS VISIONS

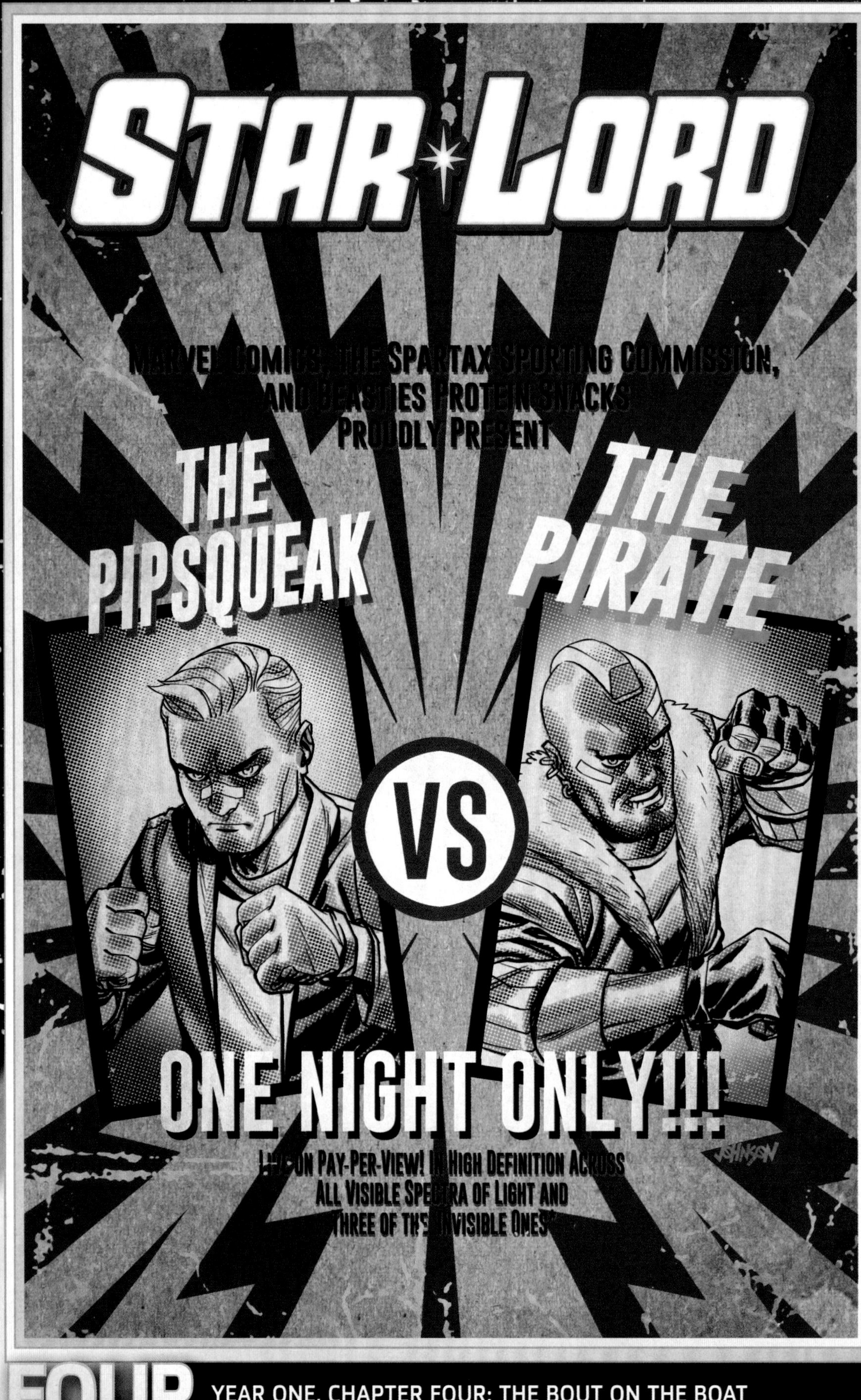

STAR-LORD

Marvel Comics, the Spartax Sporting Commission,
and Beasties Protein Snacks
Proudly Present

THE PIPSQUEAK

VS

THE PIRATE

ONE NIGHT ONLY!!!

Live on Pay-Per-View! In High Definition Across
All Visible Spectra of Light and
Three of the Invisible Ones*

JOHNSON

FOUR

YEAR ONE, CHAPTER FOUR: THE BOUT ON THE BOAT

THE ASTERION ONE.
EARTH'S FIRST OFF-WORLD COLONY MISSION.
ASTERION ONE
EXTERIOR HATCH 47-B
HISTORY IN THE MAKING.
AN EPIC ACCOMPLISHMENT.
USE WRENCH HERE TO ACTIVATE HATCH ACCESS
ALL THE HOPES OF HUMANITY COLLECTED TOGETHER INTO ONE SHIP--

--FOR ME TO ROB, CHEAT, AND STEAL.
HI, IT'S ME, PETER QUILL, TRAITOR TO SEVEN BILLION HUMANS OF EARTH.
NO BIG DEAL.

BUT I PROMISE IT'S FOR A GOOD CAUSE.
AIRLOCK EXTERIOR HATCH 47-B
FUDD
FREEZE!
REAL SLICK, QUILL.
HUH. HOW LONG HAS IT BEEN SINCE I'VE SEEN ONE OF THESE?
PING

HANDS UP!

FREEZE! OR I'LL--

NO.

OH, NO.
IT'S LISA.
WHO ARE YOU?
WHAT THE HELL ARE YOU DOING ON MY SHIP?
SECURITY FORCES ARE ALREADY EN ROUTE. LOWER YOUR WEAPON AND REMOVE YOUR MASK.
NOW!
MY MOM'S BEST FRIEND. PRACTICALLY MY AUNT.
AND COMMANDER OF THE SHIP I JUST STOLE.
THAT'S A START.
NOW THE MASK. SLOWLY.
I FEEL LIKE HIDING AND DYING AND PUKING ALL AT ONCE.
SHE'S THE LAST PERSON I WANT TO SEE ME LIKE THIS--
COMMANDER CHANG, COME IN! WE'RE BEING BOARDED BY PIRATES!
HOW--? BUT THE SHIELDS--
SOMEONE DISABLED THEM, WE'RE--OH GOD--THEY'VE GOT GUNS! AND--THEY'RE UGLY!
CHANG
I NEED ANSWERS, RIGHT NOW! WHO IS HIJACKING MY SHIP?
OH KAY, ASTERION ONE, LISTEN UP--

CHANG

YOU'RE BEING BOARDED BY THE RAVAGERS!

FOR THE LAST TIME--
--THE ASTERION ONE IS ON A MISSION OF PEACE.
POINTING YOUR GUNS AT UNARMED ASTRONAUTS JUST MAKES YOU LOOK LIKE YOU'VE GOT A LOT TO COMPENSATE FOR.

TOO TRUE. MY CREW IS NUMEROUS AND GREEDY AND THEY ALL NEED COMPENSATIN'.
NOW, COMMANDER CHANG--SURRENDER YOUR SHIP, AND I GUARANTEE THE LIVES OF YOUR CREW.
FAIR DEAL?
NO.
BUT I ACCEPT.
LISTEN UP, MUD APES! MY NAME IS YONDU, AND I'M IN CONTROL NOW!
WE'RE TAKING YOUR WARP CORES AND LEAVING YOU TO DRIFT. YOUR FATE IS IN THE HANDS OF THE STARS.
HIGH AND DRY. THAT'S THE PIRATE WAY.
THIS IS OUR SHIP NOW!
YEEE HAWWW!
YEE HAW.
WHOOP DE DOO.

AY, PETEY, YOU LEAVE YOUR CELEBRATION SPIRIT BACK ON THE SHIP?
YONDU, REMEMBER, DON'T USE MY NAME AROUND THEM--
AW, WHAT THE HELL DO YOU CARE ABOUT THESE KRUTAKERS? DIDN'T THEY KICK YOU OFF THIS MISSION?
DIDN'T THEY SAY YOU DIDN'T HAVE WHAT IT TAKES TO MAKE IT IN SPACE? WELL, TIME TO RUB THEIR NOSES IN IT!
DON'T FORGET--
--YOUR BIGGEST WISH IS ABOUT TO COME TRUE.
A DEAL IS A DEAL. WE GOT OUR SHIP, YOU'LL GET YOURS.
ONCE WE'VE MADE OUR GETAWAY, THIS BELONGS TO YOU. YOU'LL FINALLY GET REVENGE FOR THE DEATH OF YOUR PRETTY LITTLE MAMA--
YEAH, YEAH, AS IF YOU REALLY CARE ABOUT MY MOM, YOU JUST CARE THAT I GET YOU THIS DAMN--
THIS JOB AIN'T OVER YET! AND UNTIL IT IS I NEED YOU TO PULL IT TOGETHER!
NOW GO WAVE YOUR GUN AT THOSE PILOTS BEFORE I LEAVE YOU HIGH AND DRY!
OH, GREAT.
MY BEST FRIENDS FROM EARTH, ISAAC AND HASTINGS.
I'M SURE THEY'VE BEEN MISSING ME.

THESE GUYS TREATED ME LIKE GARBAGE.
YONDU AND THE PIRATES TOOK ME IN.
I'M ONE OF THEM NOW. I HELPED THEM TAKE THIS SHIP.
SO WHY DOES MY STOMACH FEEL AS SOUR AS A BAG OF LEMONS?
OKAY, DON'T GIVE ME AN EXCUSE TO GET ROUGH, SCRUBS!
MAYBE I WILL! IF YOU THINK YOU'RE UP TO IT.
LET'S SEE HOW TOUGH YOU ARE WITHOUT THAT GUN!
PLEASE GIVE ME AN EXCUSE TO GET ROUGH.
COULDN'T HACK IT IN SPACE SO YOU HAD TO STEAL SOMEONE ELSE'S SHIP?
YOU DON'T HAVE WHAT IT TAKES TO FLY THIS THING ANYWAY!
THERE WE GO.
I'M A BETTER PILOT THAN YOU, DIRTBAG!
HEY!
I PUNCHED ISAAC BEFORE.
FELT GOOD.

REAL GOOD.
I BET TAKING IT TO THE NEXT LEVEL WOULD FEEL EVEN BETTER.
HEY-- LET GO OF ME--!
STOP!
HEY, UHHHH-- YOU!
I SAID NO TROUBLE!
STAND DOWN! STAND--
KRAK
HASTINGS
KZZZZK
NO--MY MASK--
NO!

NO WAY-- UNREAL!
IT'S THE COWARD MECHANIC FROM EARTH!
PETER QUILL? EXPLAIN YOURSELF!
PETER! YOU'RE ALIVE! I CAN'T BELIEVE IT, YOU'RE--
ENOUGH!

"OOOH, AAAH, IT'S PETEY QUILL!"
BIG DEAL. THIS CHANGES ABSOLUTELY NOTHING!
SIDDOWN AND SHADDAP OR YOUR COMMANDER GETS IT!
BACK OFF, YONDU, DON'T HURT HER OR I'LL--
PETER! DON'T--
OR WHAT, YOUNG TIGER?
OR YOU'LL POLISH EVERY DECK IN THIS SHIP? YOU'RE JUST THE JANITOR, BOY, DON'T FORGET YOUR PLACE!
BACK YOURSELF DOWN OR I WON'T HESITATE TO DO IT FOR YOU!

"JUST THE JANITOR."
I'M JUST THE JANITOR.
BOSS!

THIS ONE WON'T SIMMER DOWN!
NOW!
HIT THE WARP, ISAAC--!
THOK

I'LL TAKE CARE OF YOU IN A SECOND, PETEY--
HEY THERE, LITTLE LADY!
LOOK, THAT FIRST PUNCH YOU THREW? FAIR PLAY. I MEAN, WHO HASN'T WANTED TO SMACK PETER ONCE OR TWICE... OR TWENTY TIMES?

BUT NOW, I GOTTA KEEP THE PEACE.
OOOF--!
THWAK
LOOK, GUYS. I USED TO WAKE UP EVERY DAY, AND MY ONLY GOAL WAS TO BE A PAIN IN THE ASS TO EVERYONE AROUND ME.
BUT THEN I DISCOVERED THE CUDDLY, HAPPY YONDU WITHIN ME. AND NOW I AM IN PERFECT, SERENE HARMONY WITH THE UNIVERSE.
HOWEVER, DESPITE MY PATIENT, TRANQUIL DEMEANOR, I HOPE I HAVE MADE IT ABUNDANTLY CLEAR--
I WILL NOT HESITATE TO KILL EACH AND EVERY ONE OF YOU!
I RUN THIS KRUTAKING SHIP NOW! AND NOTHING, ABSOLUTELY NOTHING, HAPPENS WITHOUT MY SAY!
I NEED MY BEASTIES--
BOSS!
NOFF NOW!
BUT HE'S GONE, BOSS!
PETER QUILL IS GONE!

WAIT--
WAIT--
PETER, STOP! WHAT ARE YOU DOING?
I'M... SAVING YOUR LIFE?
NO, I MEAN...WHAT ARE YOU DOING OUT HERE... IN SPACE? WITH PIRATES?
I, UH-- SCREW THOSE GUYS. I'M JUST THE JANITOR. APPARENTLY.
PETER--
I DON'T CARE. I'M SO GLAD YOU'RE ALIVE.
I THINK IT'S BEEN A WHOLE MONTH SINCE I'VE HAD A HUG.
THANKS... I--I'M GLAD YOU'RE ALIVE, TOO.
COME ON--WE CAN SAVE THE ASTERION IF--
UH, ABSOLUTELY NOT, WE'RE STEALING THE PIRATE SHIP AND GETTING OUT OF HERE BEFORE THEY REALIZE--
NO!
NO?
YES!
BUT THE ASTERION--
I'M NOT PART OF THE ASTERION MISSION ANYMORE, REMEMBER, "COMMANDER CHANG"? YOU FIRED ME--
PETER. I KNOW. I'M SORRY. BUT WE NEED YOU-- THE ASTERION IS IMPORTANT--

LISA, GET REAL.
THE ASTERION IS DUNZO. THE MISSION IS OVER! YOU COULDN'T TAKE IT BACK IF--
THE RAVAGERS-- THOSE GUYS ARE PIRATES, FOR REAL. THEY TAKE ANYTHING THEY WANT FROM ANY SHIP ACROSS SEVEN GALAXIES.
SOUNDS LIKE YOU ADMIRE THEM.
I LEARNED WHAT I NEEDED TO KNOW AND TOOK WHAT I WANTED FROM THEM.
NOW WE'RE GOING TO STEAL THEIR SHIP AND--
I AM NOT LEAVING MY SHIP AND MY CREW BEHIND. YOU KNOW ME BETTER THAN THAT.
IT'S NOT JUST ABOUT THAT-- LOOK.
I SWIPED IT FROM YONDU ON THE BRIDGE. HE DID A GOOD JOB TEACHING ME HOW TO PICK A POCKET.
IT'S A TRACKING GEM. DON'T YOU RECOGNIZE THE SHIP?
LISA--WE'RE REALLY GOING TO DO IT. WE'RE GOING TO GET THE ALIENS THAT KILLED MOM!

OH, PETER...
I'M SO SORRY. I'VE FAILED YOU.

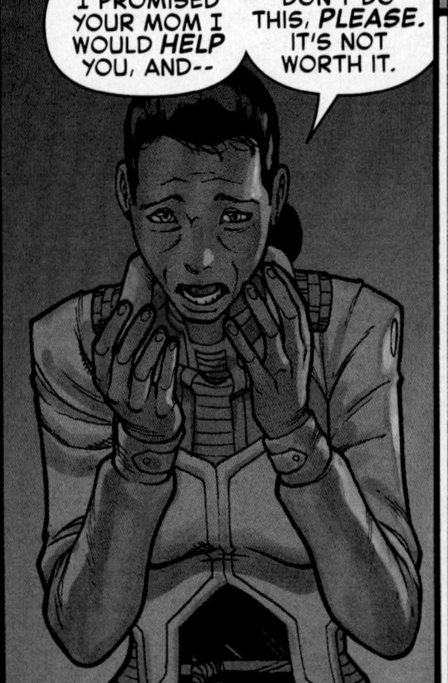
I PROMISED YOUR MOM I WOULD HELP YOU, AND--
DON'T DO THIS, PLEASE. IT'S NOT WORTH IT.

WHAT?! THIS IS THE ONLY THING WORTH ANYTHING!
SHE WAS MY MOM! I'LL DO WHATEVER IT TAKES TO--

YOU THINK YOU'RE THE ONLY ONE THAT GRIEVED FOR HER? SHE WAS LIKE MY SISTER! YOU'RE WASTING YOUR LIFE ON REVENGE AND THAT WOULD HAVE BROKEN HER HEART!
WAKE UP, PETER! GET YOUR HEAD OUT OF YOUR--

YOU KNOW WHAT? NEVER MIND.
I HAVE A JOB TO DO.
COME WITH ME. WE CAN FIX THIS. THE ASTERION-- IF YOU SHOW ME HOW TO UNLOCK THE ENGINES, I CAN--

LISA. THEY'LL KILL YOU.
THINK OF YOUR OWN LIFE.

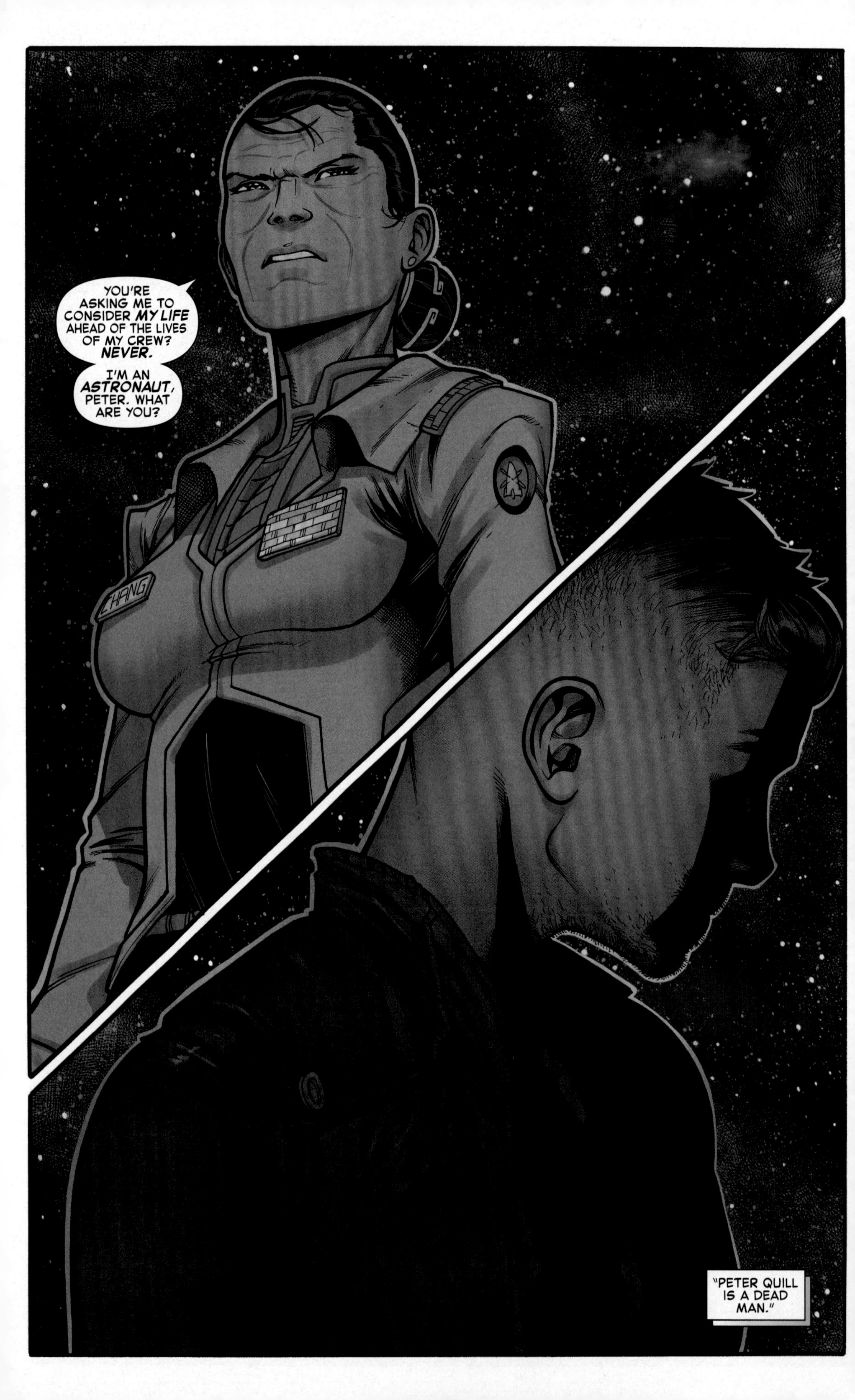
YOU'RE ASKING ME TO CONSIDER MY LIFE AHEAD OF THE LIVES OF MY CREW? NEVER.
I'M AN ASTRONAUT, PETER. WHAT ARE YOU?
C. HANG
"PETER QUILL IS A DEAD MAN."

I'LL SKIN HIM, THEN I'LL KILL HIM.
I'LL SKIN HIM, ROLL HIM IN HABANERO SAUCE, THEN I'LL KILL HIM.
WE FOUND HER WANDERING THE HALLS.
WELL, COMMANDER? WHERE'S OUR FAVORITE MUD BOY PETEY?
HE TRIED TO TAKE ME HOSTAGE. I KICKED AWAY AND ESCAPED.
HE PUT MY CREW IN DANGER, AND I WON'T HAVE THAT.
"DUTY FIRST," EH? YOU KNOW WHAT, COMMANDER? I THINK I ACTUALLY BELIEVE YOU.
YOU HEAR THAT, YOU GOONS? PETEY'S SOMEWHERE ON THIS SHIP. GO FIND HIM!
COMMANDER! THANK GOD YOU'RE--
NEVER MIND ME, IS EVERYONE OKAY?
WE'RE FIVE BY FIVE. SO, WHAT'S THE PLAN WITH QUILL?
IS HE HIDING? IS HE PLANNING A SNEAK ATTACK? IS HE RESTORING THE ENGINES?
NO...
CHANG

"...HE'S RUNNING AWAY."

YEAR ONE, CHAPTER FIVE: FROM THE EARTH TO THE STAR-LORD

FIVE

ALL MY LIFE I DREAMED OF GOING TO SPACE--FOR **REVENGE**.
NOW THAT I'M HERE, I'VE LEARNED THAT THE ONLY WAY TO SURVIVE IS TO TAKE **WHAT** YOU CAN, **WHEN** YOU CAN.
THE ALIENS THAT KILLED MY MOM...THEY'RE WITHIN MY GRASP.
AND THE *ASTERION ONE?* THEY KICKED ME OUT. RIDICULED ME.
THEY LAUNCHED A SHIP WITH A HUNDRED HUMANS ON IT, THINKING THEY COULD JUST GO COLONIZE A PLANET WITHOUT ANY TROUBLE.
IDIOTS. THIS IS SPACE. YOU HAVE TO TAKE WHAT YOU WANT.
I TOOK THIS TRACKING GEM FROM YONDU. IF HE AND THE PIRATES CATCH ME, THEY'LL KILL ME.
I'M RUNNING OUT OF TIME.
THE *ASTERION ONE*--THEY'RE NOT MY PROBLEM. THEY'RE ON THEIR OWN.
RIGHT?
I'VE GOT THINGS TO DO.
I'VE BEEN WAITING FOR THIS CHANCE FOR YEARS. IT MIGHT NOT COME AGAIN.
OKAY.
TIME TO GET TO WORK.
"HE HAS THE GEM!"

HE MUST HAVE GRABBED THE GEM OFF ME!
A DEAL IS A DEAL! AND HE JUST WENT BACK ON A DEAL!
YONDU-- BOSS--
YOU DON'T GET IT! THAT MEANS--
THAT COWARD! QUILL TOOK THEIR SHIP AND HE'S NOT COMING BACK!
THAT'S RIGHT, ISAAC. WE CAN'T COUNT ON HIS HELP. WE NEED TO UNLOCK THE ENGINES--
COMMANDER CHANG, IF YOU MAKE A DISTRACTION, I THINK I CAN HACK THE ENGINES ONLINE--
PETEY AIN'T HERE ON THE ASTERION ONE.
THAT GEM IS ALL HE WANTED. HIS LITTLE DIRT-BOY DREAMS ARE ABOUT TO COME TRUE. WITH THE GEM, HE CAN TRACK DOWN THE BADOON SHIP AND--
HE'S OUT THERE, ON OUR SHIP.
WE BEEN LOOKING IN THE WRONG PLACE--
YONDU-- LOOK!
MY... GOLD?
QUILL!
I'M GONNA KILL YOU!

HOW DO YOU GET UNDER A PIRATE'S SKIN?
YOU MESS WITH THEIR TREASURE.
WHAT AM I DOING? I DON'T EVEN KNOW.

I'M TRYING TO SAVE THE *ASTERION ONE*. AND THEN I'LL GO AFTER THE BADOON THAT KILLED MY MOM.
IF I'M LUCKY.
I KNOW, I KNOW. I SHOULD BE LONG GONE. WHO'S THE IDIOT NOW?
WELP. TOO LATE NOW, PROBABLY...
OUR TREASURE!
OUR BEAUTIFUL GOLD!
NO! THIS CAN'T BE HAPPENING!
TO THE SHIP! TO THE SHIP!
I WISH I HAD MORE TIME TO WORK ON THIS BABY.
FREDDIE BACK IN THE MECHANIC POOL WOULD MAKE SO MUCH FUN OF ME FOR THIS SKETCHY MOD.
I GOTTA HURRY TO THE ENGINE ROOM--
RUN!
WE CAN STILL GET SOME OF IT BACK!
GET OUT OF MY WAY!
YOU'RE SLOWING ME DOWN!
YOU DUMB KRUTAKERS! **GET BACK HERE!**
THIS IS A ***TRAP!*** SOMEONE STAY BACK AND HOLD DOWN THE *ASTERION ONE!*
DON'T MAKE ME DRAG YOU BACK HERE!

OH, FLARK, THEY'RE ALREADY ON BOARD!
TOO MUCH TO DO, GOTTA KEEP THEM OUTTA MY HAIR...
THE TREASURE! IT'S ALL GONE!
IT CAN'T BE!
ALL THOSE JOBS, ALL THOSE HEISTS!
HOW-- HOW DID--
>SOB< MY RETIREMENT!
THOOM
WHAT?
IT'S LOCKED!
PUNCH IT OPEN!
YOU PUNCH IT OPEN!
I DON'T WANNA DIE IN HERE!
THAT DOOR'S PRETTY HARD-CORE, SHOULD HOLD THEM LONG ENOUGH.
(I HOPE THAT WAS ALL OF THEM.)
THE ENGINE ROOM IS WHAT I REALLY NEED--
DAMN IT-- QUILL!
I'M GONNA KILL EVERYONE!
HASTINGS! GO!

OKAY, FROM DOWN HERE IN THE ENGINE ROOM I CAN PERFORM FLIGHT CONTROLS...KINDA.
NO TIME TO MAKE CALCULATIONS.
THIS IS LIKE DRIVING A CAR FROM UNDER THE HOOD WITH A PHONE. WHILE BLINDFOLDED.
GOTTA GUESS--HOW MUCH THRUSTER IS TOO MUCH THRUSTER?
EENY, MEENY, MINEY--
BLAST THE THRUSTERS! GO!
KATHOOM
OKAY, THAT WAS WAY TOO MUCH.
ARE WE... MOVING?
RRRRRRRUMBLE
WHO THE HELL LIT THE CANDLES?!
THE PIRATE SHIP IS *LEAVING?!*
WHY ARE THEY *TAKING OFF?*
HASTINGS! *WE NEED ENGINES!*
I'M HURRYING!

THE SHIP IS MOVING FAST. WE'RE LEAVING THE ASTERION BEHIND.
I AM OFFICIALLY OUT OF TIME.
KRSSSSSH
NO TIME TO GET FANCY.
EMERGENCY FUEL EJECT
EMERGENCY FUEL EJECT ENGAGED.
SCHUNK
GOTTA LEAVE THESE GUYS HIGH AND DRY.
IT'S THE PIRATE WAY.
ENGINES ARE ONLINE!
GREAT WORK, HASTINGS!
COMMANDER! THIS IS OUR CHANCE!
HOLD ENGINES! THIS IS PETER'S DOING. IT MUST BE! HE CAN STILL ESCAPE--
YONDU-- OPEN THE DOOR--
LEMME OUTTA HERE!
CALM DOWN IN THERE, I'M THINKIN'!
PETEY-- YOU AIN'T AS SMART AS YOU THINK YOU ARE...
I KNOW WHERE YOU'RE GOING...
"...AND I'M COMIN' FOR YA!"
TWO OBJECTS IN A VACUUM, ONE MOVING AWAY FROM THE OTHER. RATE, SPEED, DISTANCE.
I HAVE TO SHOOT MYSELF AT THE ASTERION WITH THE RIGHT AMOUNT OF FORCE.
IT'S JUST A SIMPLE PHYSICS PROBLEM.

TOO BAD I SUCK AT MATH.
Star-Lord
KLIK
BABY, DON'T FAIL ME NOW.
Star-Lord
HERE WE GO--
FWOOOSH

ONE SMALL STEP FOR A JANITOR...
...ONE GIANT LEAP FOR A STAR-LORD!

OH, GOD
OH, GOD--
THE ASTERION IS MOVING TOO FAST!
THERE HE IS!
IS THAT... A VACUUM CLEANER?!
FLY, QUILL! FLY!
YOU WERE RIGHT--QUILL SAVED THE ASTERION ONE!
THAT STEELY-EYED MISSILE MAN!
IF I THROW MY WEIGHT TO THE LEFT, EASE UP ON THE THRUSTERS--
WHAT THE--?
YONDU!
NO!
PETER!
THAT BLUE BASTARD!
HE CAN'T GET FREE!
HE'S SLOWING DOWN!

NO!
HE'S SLOWING ME DOWN!

I DID IT!
I'M FREE!
HIT THE THRUSTERS--
--I CAN STILL--
--WAIT--
WHY'S HE SMILING, THAT ARROGANT BLUEBERRY--
OH, NO.
HE'S GOT THE GEM, HE'S--
NO NO DON'T LET GO PLEASE DON'T--
THAT BASTARD. HE'S GONNA MAKE ME CHOOSE?
I CAN-- IF I REACH OUT--

PLEASE.

IF I CAN--
THIS IS EVERYTHING-- THIS IS--
NO.
THERE'S MORE THAN THIS.
PICK A HIGH TARGET AND YOU WILL HIT IT, PETER.
WHO ARE YOU, PETER?
I CAN BE MORE THAN THIS.
MY MOM GAVE HER LIFE TO GIVE ME A CHANCE.
I CAN'T BLOW IT LIKE THIS.
I WON'T-- AH!

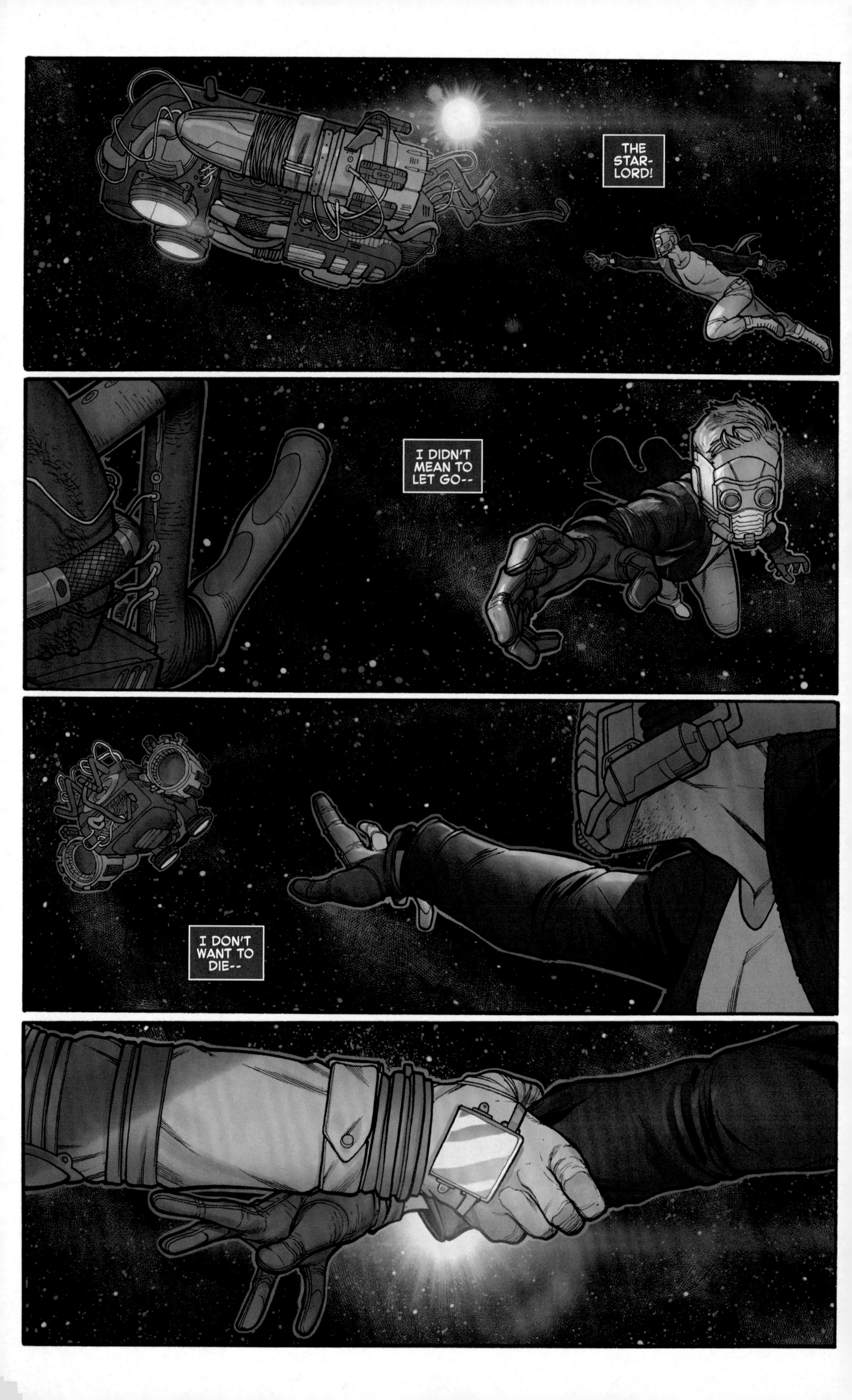
THE STAR-LORD!
I DIDN'T MEAN TO LET GO--
I DON'T WANT TO DIE--

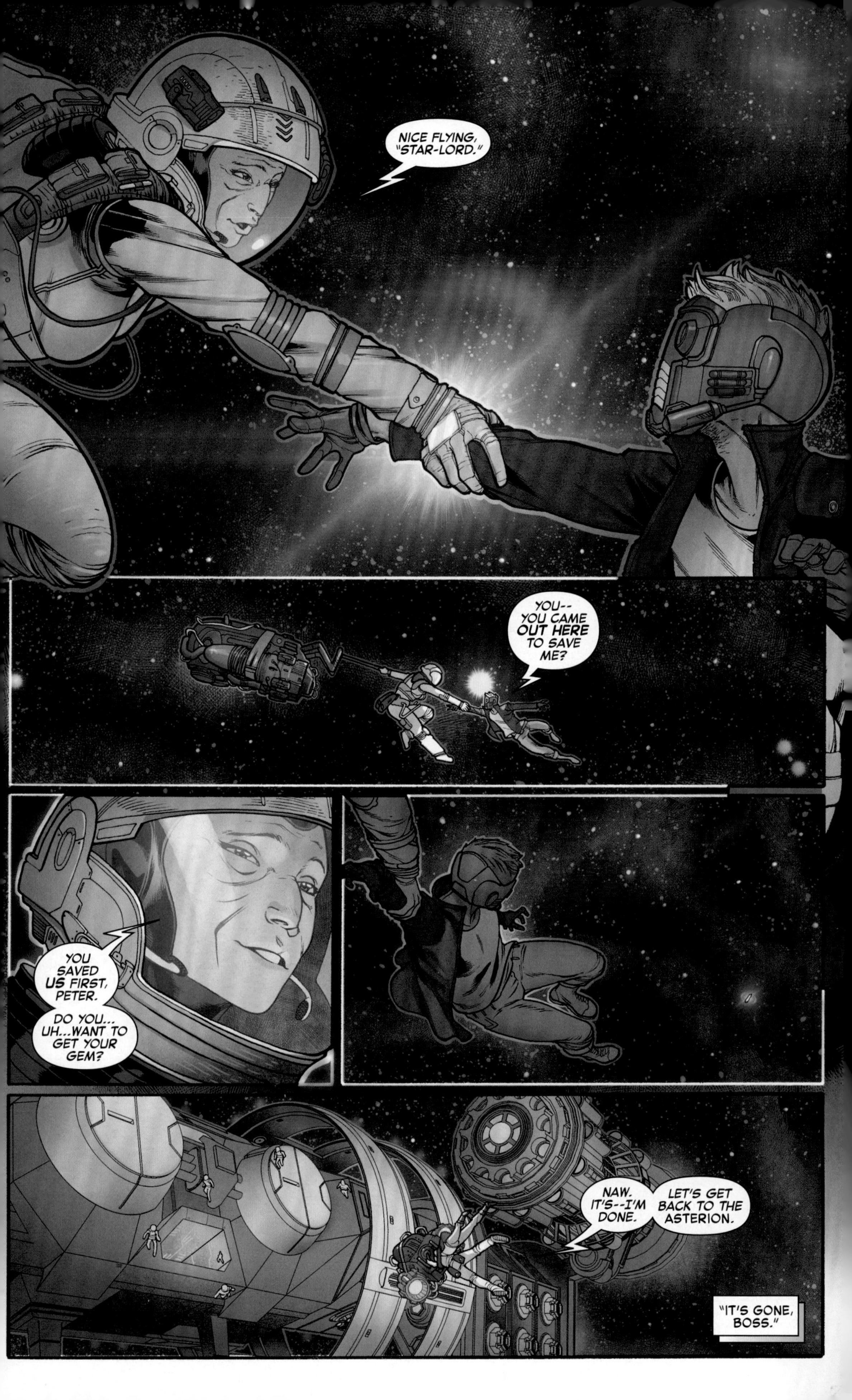
NICE FLYING, "STAR-LORD."
YOU-- YOU CAME OUT HERE TO SAVE ME?
YOU SAVED US FIRST, PETER.
DO YOU... UH...WANT TO GET YOUR GEM?
NAW. IT'S--I'M DONE.
LET'S GET BACK TO THE ASTERION.
"IT'S GONE, BOSS."

THE ASTERION ONE IS GONE.
WE CAN'T PURSUE IT BECAUSE QUILL DUMPED OUR FUEL.
HE LEFT US HIGH AND DRY.
OUR, UH, FATE IS IN THE HANDS OF THE STARS NOW. IT'S THE--
YES, I KNOW IT'S THE PIRATE WAY, YOU IDIOT!
THAT DAMN VACUUM CLEANER.
WELL, PETEY...WE MADE YOU INTO A GOOD PIRATE AFTER ALL.
TOO GOOD, IT SEEMS.
LISTEN UP!
SCRAPE TOGETHER WHAT'S LEFT OF THE TREASURE. AS SOON AS WE GET TO CIVILIZATION, WE'RE PLACING A BOUNTY ON THE HEAD OF PETER QUILL.
AFTER ALL...THE GALAXY IS A VERY SMALL PLACE.

PLANET XERXES.
ASTERION COLONY.
A PERMANENT COLONY ON ANOTHER PLANET.
THIS IS HISTORIC, PETER. AND YOU HAD A HAND IN IT.
I'M SORRY I KICKED YOU OFF THE MISSION. CLEARLY WE NEEDED YOU...
LISA--
--I'M SORRY. FOR WHAT I SAID TO YOU ABOUT MOM.
PETER, IT'S OKAY.
WHEN I STOPPED GRIEVING AND STOPPED BEING ANGRY...THAT'S WHEN I FIRST STARTED PLANNING THIS MISSION.
EIGHT YEARS, FROM MY KITCHEN TABLE TO THE STARS.
YOU WILL ALWAYS HAVE A PLACE IN THIS COLONY. YOU SURE YOU WON'T STAY?
I'LL VISIT.
HOW OFTEN?
I WILL! I'LL VISIT, I SWEAR!

THEY SAY SPACE IS A MIRROR. WE DON'T DISCOVER THE UNIVERSE, WE DISCOVER OURSELVES.
NOW GO...FIND YOURSELF.
THANK YOU.
WHAT'S SO FUNNY? I'M TRYING TO BE INSPIRING!
NOTHING. IT'S JUST--
--NO OFFENSE, LISA, BUT I HAD FUN STEALING YOUR SHIP.
WELL, I HOPE YOU HAD JUST AS MUCH FUN STEALING IT BACK.
WHERE TO NOW, "STAR-LORD"?

IT'S A BIG GALAXY.
I'M GONNA GO SEE WHAT IT HAS IN STORE FOR ME.
TOOK ME FIFTY BILLION LIGHT-YEARS TO FIGURE OUT WHAT I WANT TO BE WHEN I GROW UP.

I WAS AN OKAY ASTRONAUT, AT BEST.

AND I WAS KIND OF A RIDICULOUS PIRATE.

BUT TOGETHER, I CAN BE SOMETHING BETTER.

I CAN BE THE LEGENDARY

STAR-LORD

THE END

#1 HIP-HOP VARIANT
BY TRADD MOORE AND VAL STAPLES

#1 VARIANT BY YASMINE PUTRI